Girlz Have Voices Books

REBEL OF THE RHODES

Other Books in the REBEL OF THE RHODES *Series*

REBEL OF THE RHODES: Forsaken Flame
REBEL OF THE RHODES: Guerillas and Love
REBEL OF THE RHODES: The Liberation Struggle

Girlz Have Voices Books

REBEL OF THE RHODES
Forbidden Flame

Palesa R. Denga

Darling Kind Publishing
An Imprint of TatendaCharlesMunyuki Publishing

REBEL OF THE RHODES: Forbidden Flame

Girlz Have Voices Books

All rights reserved; no part of this publication may be reproduced or transmitted by means, electronic, mechanical, photocopying or otherwise without the prior permission of the publisher.

First published in Zimbabwe in 2025
Darling Kind Publishing
an imprint of Tatenda Charles Munyuki Publishing

Copyright © Palesa R. Denga 2025
Cover Illustration Copyright © Straightline Designz 2025
Cover illustration by Straightline Designz 2025

The moral rights of the author have been asserted

ISBN   9780797465817

Typeset, printed and bound by Darling Kind Publishing,
Harare, Zimbabwe.
darlingkindp@live.com

facebook.com/girlzhavevoices

I dedicate this book to all the rebels who refuse to let society define them…

Dear Reader

This isn't just ink on paper.
It's the scream of a generation silenced by centuries. It's the cry of children torn from their mothers by iron chains of slavery. It's the sobs of fathers who watched their lands stolen, renamed and drained of its dignity. It's the lullaby of grandparents who whispered into the dark, only for their stories to be swallowed by smoke and gunfire. These stories are fragments of bloodied truths collected from the edges of Africa's broken mirrors.
We write of marriage, not just as a union of love, but as a battlefield where culture, gender and power collide.
We write of colonialism, not as history, but as a haunting horror that still rattles our bones and reshapes our reflections.
We write of racism, not as a concept, but as a living wound carved into our skins, whispered in boardrooms and screamed at borders.
We write of love that blooms in the shadows of war, and hate that poisons even the soil beneath our feet.
We write of despair when hope feels like a foreign tongue.
We write of segregation, not only in the street, but in the mind.
We call on our ancestors, not just for guidance, but for forgiveness.
We expose violence, we unveil brutality, we mourn the price of war.
We mourn the slow and silent death of culture that has been diluted, dismissed and devoured.
We speak of slavery, not as a past tense, but as legacy etched into names we were forced to carry and dreams we were forced to bury, but above all, we write of Africa.
The Africa that bleeds, sings, rises and remembers.
The Africa that was never poor, only pillaged.
The Africa that has never stopped fighting for the right to tell its own story.
This historical fiction isn't a book. It's a resurrection and, as you turn each page, I ask only one thing,
Feel it.
Let it move you.
Let it break you.
Let it remind you that we are still here.
Still writing.
Still rising.
For Africa.

With hope,
Palesa R. Denga

REBEL HEART

The sun rose over the valley, casting a warm golden colour across the thatched rooftops of the village. The village was surrounded by mountains and cloaked in dense forests.

Life moved slowly there. No one had ever left the village – that's what they said. Even the birds, they said, always came back before sunset. Even the river never dared to run too far. The villagers farmed, practiced pastoralism, laughed and lived as if history had never come knocking.

No one spoke of the *First Chimurenga War*. They had heard no news of the wars that raged beyond their mountains, of the armies that marched and the battles that were fought. They knew nothing of the colonizers who had come to their land, bringing with them strange customs and foreign ways. No one knew about the *Union Jack* that was now planted in their soil. They had no idea that their country was being shaped by the forces of history – that empires were rising and falling. They didn't know that the world was being forever altered. All they knew was the simple and peaceful life they lived.

Inside a small hut, eighteen-year-old Chiedza stirred beneath a worn goat fur covering. She blinked at the sunlight slipping through the crack in the dagga wall. Her muscles ached, not from work, but from her father's expectations that governed her life. Her father was a strict man who believed in traditional ways and expected all his three daughters to behave like proper young women.

She stepped out of her hut and went to the kitchen. Her mother, Tamburai, in her early forties, was already up and about in the kitchen, stirring a pot of pap over the fire. Her stomach growled with hunger as she watched her mother work.

'Good morning, *Amai*,' she said, going over to give her mother a hug.

'Good morning, *mwanangu*,' her mother replied smiling. 'I made your favourite food – sadza, with pumpkin leaves.'

'*Maitabasa, Amai*,' she grinned, and dropped onto the reed mat.

Just then, her father, Mhondi, in his mid-forties, came into the hut, with a stern and disapproving look.

'Chiedza, you woke up late, again? How many times must I tell you that a woman must not wake up late? Do you expect me to do your chores for you?' Mhondi scolded her.

She hastily got to her feet. Her eyes were cast downward in a gesture of submission. 'I'm sorry, *Baba*,' she muttered.

'Sorry isn't enough, Chiedza,' he growled. 'A woman must be diligent and hardworking. She must wake up with the sun and complete her chores before the day is old. You aren't a child anymore and it's time you learnt to take responsibility for yourself.'

Chiedza bit her tongue. She felt frustrated, but she knew it was better not to express it. She knew arguing with him would only lead to more trouble so she nodded meekly and kept her eyes downcast as Mhondi sat on his stool.

There was silence in the hut as Tamburai served breakfast. The fire cracked, but no one spoke as they ate. When the meal was done, Mhondi rose.

'I'm going to chop firewood,' he said.

He turned and walked out of the hut, leaving Chiedza and her mother to their thoughts. The door creaked shut behind him and they both felt relieved. Chiedza let out a soft sigh and her mother looked up. After clearing the plates, her mother told her to bring in the firewood her father was chopping outside.

Outside, the wood lay in a neat pile, but her father was nowhere to be seen. She crouched beside it, running her hands over the rough barks, but her mind was far away, lost in thoughts of a life beyond the chores and duties she was expected to fulfil. She knew what was expected of her and yet, with each passing day, she found herself questioning it more. *Why should girls be bound by these rules?* She carried the firewood inside and sat in a corner, still deep in her thoughts.

Tamburai watched her for a moment. Her smile grew faint as she caught the faraway look in Chiedza's eyes. '*Mwanangu*,' she said gently. 'I know you dream of more, but the world isn't kind to girls. You must know your place. Your father has plans for you.'

'Plans?' Chiedza asked.

'Yes,' her mother replied, lowering her voice as though to keep the words from carrying too far. 'You are to marry the chief's son. It's the way things are done. It will bring honour to our family. I have been taunted all these years for not being able to bear a son for your father.' Her eyes looked over her daughter, measuring her reaction carefully.

The chief's son? Chiedza had heard whispers for weeks about the chief's son's search for a suitable wife and she hadn't expected he was going to choose her. The idea seemed so foreign, yet so real.

'But... why?' she asked.

Tamburai hesitated, 'It's the way things are, *mwanangu*,' she said. 'The chief's son likes you and so you must not question it. Both your sisters are married and now it's your turn. If you marry the chief's son, I will no longer be taunted and teased by the other villagers for not giving birth to a boy. They will look up to me with respect and our family will be held in high esteem.'

'Why do I have to be forced to marry him just because he likes me?' Chiedza asked. 'Why can't I choose my own husband or choose not to marry at all? Or we can just run away, *Amai*. Yes, let us leave this village and all its unfairness behind. We can start afresh away from this village.'

'You know we can't leave this village, Chiedza,' Tamburai said. 'There's nowhere else to go and, besides, our ancestors warned us not to leave. They said that whoever leaves will perish and that there are only monsters and dangers outside our village.'

'How do you know that, *Amai*?' Chiedza asked. 'Have you ever left the village or do you know anyone who has?'

Her mother's face went pale and she shook her head. 'No, *mwanangu*, I have never left the village and I don't know anyone who has, but we must listen to our ancestors and do as they say. It's not safe to leave.'

Chiedza didn't want be forced to marry a man she didn't love.

'Let's just go and find out for ourselves, *Amai*,' she said. 'I don't believe all those stories. They're just made up to keep us trapped in this village. Let's go and see what's out there and make our own decisions.'

'No – we will not leave the village and you shall not disobey me. It's not safe and it's not right. You must forget this foolish idea and prepare to marry the chief's son as is expected of you.'

'Okay, *Amai*.'

'Promise me, Chiedza. Swear on me and on our ancestors that you shall not run away,' her mother pleaded.

'I swear on you, *Amai*, and on the spirits of our ancestors, that I will not run away from our village.'

Chiedza loved her mother dearly, but she could see the silent weariness in her eyes, the resignation that came with knowing her place, but she was different from her mother. She didn't want to be the wife of the chief's son. She didn't want to be defined by her relationship to a man or by the roles of a daughter, wife and mother that were anticipated of her as a girlchild. It wasn't that the chief's son was unattractive.

He was a handsome young man with the promise of power and status that came with his position, but to her he represented everything she despised – the rigid roles that defined her and the future that she had no say in. To her, being chosen as a wife wasn't an honour, but it was a prison. There was nothing she could do about it except getting married to a man chosen for her just like how her two older sisters had done.

Later that day, she was walking through the village when the murmur of voices caught her attention. She could hear the gossiping long before she reached the group of women gathered by the river. Their voices were low, but carried with unmistakable excitement.

'Have you heard?' one of the women whispered, her eyes darting around to make sure no one else could hear. 'The chief's son is set to marry Chiedza. It's already decided, they say.'

'She's just a girl,' another woman added. 'What does she know of the chief's ways? Of his life?'

The first woman laughed softly, with a sound that lacked real joy. 'It doesn't matter. The chief's son has chosen her. What more is there to say? She'll be a fine wife, I am sure.'

'I knew she was going to catch his eye as soon as I heard he was looking for a wife. She's without doubt the most beautiful girl in the village. She also has the brightest smile. No wonder her parents named her Chiedza,' another woman said, full of excitement.

Chiedza's smile was tight, the kind that didn't reach her eyes, as she looked at the women gossiping by the river. The words they spoke felt like a burden in her chest. *Most beautiful?* She didn't care about the praise for it was shallow and tied to expectations that she had no interest in fulfilling.

'She's a lucky girl. I really wish it was me in her place,' a girl said.

The others murmured their agreements and giggled simultaneously.

The whispers grew louder as she passed by the river unnoticed. The pressure to conform and to be what they wanted her to be was suffocating. She wanted to scream at them, to tell them that there was more to life than marriage and that girls like her could be just as special and important as boys, but she said nothing.

Would they understand? she wondered. She walked away from the river.

'The chief's son has chosen me to be his wife,' she repeated the words, silently to herself.

If that's all they see in me, a prize to be won, then what am I? she wondered. *Is this all there really is?*

She could already picture her life in the village doing the duties she was expected to do as a wife. She had seen it all around her. Her mother worked tirelessly, with no end in sight, and all the other women, as strong as they were, seemed bound to a fate they had no power to change.

Her thoughts were interrupted by the sound of a soft voice calling her name. It was Chipo, her oldest sister, whom she hadn't seen since she got married, as married women were not allowed to see their biological family unless there was a major event that brought people together. Chipo was in her early twenties, much quieter than the rest of her sisters and more thoughtful, with a gentle nature that commanded respect.

'Chiedza!' Chipo called again. Her voice was hesitant, but urgent.

Chiedza turned to see her standing just beyond the cluster of huts, with her face half-hidden by the shade of a tree

'*Sisi* Chipo,' Chiedza greeted, forcing a smile as she walked over. 'It's been a while since I have seen you. How are you?'

'It's good to see you too, little sister,' Chipo smiled weakly. 'It's been a while indeed. I am… what can I say, life is life after you get married.'

Chiedza saw the rings in her eyes. 'What's the matter?'

Chipo looked around, ensuring no one was watching them or listening 'I heard the talk by the river,' she said, her voice lowered and her eyes locked on her youngest sister's. 'You hear what they say about the chief's son and you?'

Chiedza nodded her lips pressed together. 'I heard.'

'I don't think you should let them tell you who you are, Chiedza. You're different. You've always been different. Don't let them make you believe that your life is already decided for you.'

'What can I do, *sisi*? What choice do I have?' Chiedza asked desperately.

Chipo shrugged, a small, but enigmatic smile tugging at her lips. 'Sometimes, the only way to change things is by saying a simple "no". Don't make the same mistake I did – I was too scared to say no to *Baba* and now look at how miserable my life is.'

Chiedza noticed the faint scars on her sister's cheeks.

Chipo's voice dropped to a whisper and she leaned in closer to her sister. 'In our village, we women are seen as nothing more than property. We are expected to obey our fathers, our husbands and even our own sons. We aren't allowed to make our own decisions or to have our own thoughts. We are just supposed to be silent, submissive and obedient.' Her words were laced with a deep bitterness. Chiedza could feel her sister's anger and frustration. 'Listen to me Chiedza – this isn't the way it has to be. We don't have to be bound by these oppressing rules. Let us run away together and be our own women away from this village.'

'But I'm scared,' Chiedza said. '*Amai* told me that there isn't anything, but monsters out there waiting to pounce on us if we disobey our ancestors. She says our ancestors told us not to leave our village. She also said that they will curse us if we leave and that we'll be punished for our disobedience. What if it's true, *sisi*? What if we are really not supposed to leave?'

Chipo looked at her younger sister, frustrated. '*Amai* has filled your head with those stories to keep you in line, Chiedza,' she said. 'She wants you to be afraid of the unknown and of change since she knows you are rebellious deep down, but I'm telling you those stories are not true. There are no monsters out there – I'm sure there are only people struggling to survive just like us and as for our ancestors, they may have had their reasons for creating these rules and traditions, but it doesn't mean we have to follow them blindly. We have to think for ourselves, Chiedza. We have to make our own decisions and forge our own paths.'

Chipo could see the fear in her sister's eyes. She knew that her sister had been taught to conform and never to question the status quo, but she also knew that Chiedza was different. She knew that she longed to be free, just like her.

'*Amai* wants to keep us trapped,' Chipo continued. 'She wants to keep us in this village living this traditional life because it's what she knows, but I'm telling you, *munin'ina wangu,* there's a whole world out there waiting for us to explore. We don't have to be bound by these ancient traditions and rules. We can create our own destinies, Chiedza. We can be our own women. Think about it. I will be on my way now. Let me know what you would have decided tomorrow.'

Chipo walked away leaving her sister lost in thoughts. She headed to the river to collect water and walked in the direction of her homestead. When she arrived, she found her husband, Rovai, sitting and smoking outside, under the large *mutohwe* tree. He was in his mid-twenties.

She put the clay pot full of water down before kneeling to greet her husband. '*Maswera sei, Mhofu*?' she said, clapping her hands with respect.

'Where were you?' Rovai asked. 'You've returned home late.'

'I had gone to collect water from the river, my husband,' she replied.

'Are you sure that's all you did?'

'Yes, that's all I did and returned straight home.'

'How dare you lie to me? You think I'm not aware of what you were doing under that tree near the river. You talked with your sister. Why did you talk to her?' he asked, with a cold voice.

'I… I was… j… j… just greeting her. That's all,' she stuttered.

Rovai dragged Chipo to their hut and threw her in despite her struggles to be free from his clutches. He slapped her on the face countless times and shouted accusations simultaneously, but that was the last straw – Chipo had had enough. She pushed him away from her.

'Stop it, Rovai. I can't carry on like this. You are always mistreating me every chance you get. Why? Just because I'm a woman and there's nothing I can do about it? I have had enough and I am tired of this abuse and oppression!' she shouted at him.

She had never spoken to her husband like this. She had never defied him out loud, but something inside of her was finally awakening. She was fed up of her husband's constant abuse.

He looked at her shocked. Never in his life had he ever seen nor heard a woman raise her voice at a man. With a sudden sharp motion, he raised his hand and slapped her across the face. The force of the blow sent Chipo stumbling backward. The sting on her cheek was like fire, but it wasn't the pain that hit her hardest. It was the look in Rovai's eyes, which was a cold hard glare of a man who had lost all patience with her.

'You are nothing,' he spat. 'I have given you everything and you repay me with disrespect. I took pity on you and married you. I did you a huge favour by marrying you – you ugly fool!'

Chipo started feeling angry after hearing her husband's words, but before she could do or say anything, he started beating her violently. She tried fighting back, but Rovai's strength overwhelmed her. He continued punching her and kicking her ruthlessly. She screamed in pain and begged him to stop, but he was too angry to listen. He had never felt really disrespected by a woman before hence his ego was bruised. She started spitting blood and he didn't stop even when she had stopped moving. He finally stopped after many minutes and that's when he realized Chipo was dead.

He sat on the floor beside Chipo's corpse, deep in thought, but his face showed no remorse. He believed he had done what was necessary since she had done something, which was considered uncouth for a woman to do in their village. If he had reported her to the chief, she was bound to be killed anyway.

He left her corpse on the floor and went to tell the chief what had happened. The chief, who was in his late forties and quite young than your usual age for a chief, decided it was best not to reveal what had caused Chipo's death in order to save her family's reputation since her sister was going to be married to his son. The chief knew this would create a wildfire in his kingdom, and he wasn't prepared to deal with such chaos, with only two years since he had ascended to the chiefship.

The chief sent his most trusted messenger, an elderly man in his late sixties named Nhamo, to deliver the news of Chipo's death to her family. Old Nhamo walked slowly to the family's homestead, with a heavy heart because of the burden of the message that he was going to deliver.

He found Chipo's family inside their kitchen. Tamburai was busy preparing supper in the kitchen while Chiedza helped her and Mhondi was waiting impatiently for supper to be served.

'*Tisvikewo*,' Old Nhamo shouted to announce his arrival.

Mhondi looked up and saw the old man. 'Old Nhamo, oh, it's you!' he exclaimed surprised since he knew that Old Nhamo was the chief's trusted messenger. 'What brings you here? Please, come in and sit on that stool over there.'

Old Nhamo nodded his head with gratitude and stepped inside the hut. He walked slowly scanning the room as his aged joints creaked with each step. Mhondi offered him a calabash of traditional beer when he had finally sat on the stool.

'What brings you here, Old Nhamo?' Mhondi asked once again.

Old Nhamo took a sip of the beer. 'I come bearing sad news,' he said, in a low and grave voice.

'What is it, Old Nhamo?' Mhondi asked.

Old Nhamo cleared his throat wondering how to tell them the news. 'Chipo, your eldest daughter, has passed away,' his voice cracked with emotion as he told them.

Tamburai's eyes widened in horror and she let out a bloodcurdling scream.

Chiedza stumbled backwards in shock. 'No… no… this can't be,' she whispered to herself. *'Munhu wandaona masikati afa sei?'*

She thought back to the afternoon when she had seen Chipo standing under the tree near the river. She had talked to her and Chipo even told her the plans she had to leave the village. *How could Chipo be dead? How could she die before fulfilling her desire to leave the village? Had the ancestors decided to cut her life short before she broke their rules? Were they afraid of what she was going to discover if she left the village or they just could not tolerate her brewing defiance?* The voices around her grew distant and she felt like she was in a daze. She could not process the news and refused to accept that her oldest and favourite sister was gone just like that.

Mhondi's expression didn't change, but his eyes betrayed a flicker of pain. He nodded slowly. 'I see.'

Old Nhamo's eyes dropped, unable to meet theirs. *'Nematamudziko,* but I'm not at liberty to disclose the details.'

Mhondi rose from his seat and his movements remained deliberate like a warrior steeling himself for battle. He was trying to stay calm, but deep down he was hurting. Although he had never really shown it, he loved and adored all his daughters, but he was tied to the societal expectations of how a man was supposed to behave. He was a man, after all, and men didn't show weakness. The mantra echoed in his mind, a constant reminder that had been drummed into him since childhood. He fought back the tears that threatened to come out and hastily blinked them away. He cleared his throat, the sound like a rusty gate scraping against concrete. *'Awonekwa.* Thank you, Old Nhamo,' he finally said. 'You may go.'

Old Nhamo nodded sympathetically and departed, leaving the family to their grief. The sound of his footsteps faded into the silence.

The news of Chipo's death spread in the village and the villagers began to prepare for the funeral. Women and men gathered at the family's homestead offering condolences and support. The sound of mourning and wailing was the only thing that could be heard, which was very heartbreaking since it was a devastating loss. Chipo's corpse was brought the following evening and it was covered with animal skins to hide the bruises and marks she had got from being beaten.

In accordance with traditions and customs of the village, the family started making arrangements for Chipo's funeral. The oldest man in the village whose name was Garai was notified and he began to coordinate the preparations. Everyone was dressed in the traditional mourning attires. The women cooked traditional dishes such as pap and goat's meat to feed the mourners. Chiedza and her other sister, Chisi – only a year older than her, who had come for the funeral, curled up beside their mother, shaking with sobs. They were offered food, but they had no appetite since the sorrow was too overwhelming.

At dawn, Garai led the procession to the burial site accompanied by the sound of drum and singing. As they reached the burial site, the villagers formed a semi-circle around the grave. Garai offered words of condolences and asked the ancestors to accept Chipo's soul. Her body was lowered into the ground and the men filled it with soil. As the dirt covered the body, the villagers sang and cried bidding farewell to Chipo. The funeral ceremony ended with a traditional feast where everyone gathered and shared food, stories and memories of Chipo's life. Although she was gone, her spirit lived on in the hearts of those who loved her.

SHACKLES OF TRADITION

The homestead felt empty and still the morning after Chipo's burial. The usual noise and bustle of family activity doing their respective chores in the morning was replaced by an unfathomable scary silence. In the kitchen, the cooking fire, usually ablaze by dawn, lay cold and dark. The pots, which were supposed to have been clanging with morning preparation, hung silently from the rafters untouched. Tamburai was sitting on the floor, contemplating about her eldest daughter's sudden death. Her eyes were still red, rimmed from crying ever since she had heard the horrible news of Chipo's death. Chiedza was standing in the middle of the hut, staring at her mother, unsure how to comfort her in order to decrease her grief.

Mhondi stormed into the hut. His face was twisted in anger as he started scolding them. 'What's going on in this house?' he shouted. 'Why are you two sitting around doing nothing?'

Chiedza's mother cowered. 'I… I was just taking a moment to collect myself,' she stammered.

'Collect yourself? Tsk, woman, are you out of your mind? You've been collecting yourself all morning. There's work to be done. The fields won't tend themselves.'

Mhondi was a stalwart farmer and he found solace in farming. He didn't care that his family was grieving because he didn't want to show that Chipo's death had affected him greatly. He was the head of the house and all he knew was holding power. He wouldn't hesitate to assert his dominance for he was a product of traditional masculinity and he expected his family to obey him every time he ordered them to do something.

'Get up!' he barked. 'There is work to be done. Chiedza, you will help your mother with cooking food we will eat before we go to the fields and, you,' he turned to his wife, 'you will make sure the hut is spotless. I will not have our home looking like a mess.'

Chiedza and her mother exchanged a defeated glance. They knew they had no choice, but to obey even though they had no strength to go to the fields. Chiedza reluctantly began to help her mother with the cooking. Her father's outburst had left her feeling bitter and resentful. She wondered why he was so harsh during a time when they were all hurting.

She thought about her sister Chipo while she was cooking. She could not believe that she was never going to hear Chipo's laughter ever again or see her smile and presence. She smiled to herself as she thought of when Chipo had once slapped a boy who had made promiscuous comments about her. Their father had pretended to be angry, came scolding her, and had failed to control the grin that was attempting to show on his face. They had all laughed and gossiped about how their father was secretly proud of Chipo for standing up for herself as soon as he left the hut. Chipo was a brave and confident person who had spoken whatever she wanted, but all that had stopped when she was forced to marry Rovai against her will.

Tamburai sensed Chiedza's distress. She put a gentle hand on her shoulder. '*Mwanangu*, I know it's hard, but we have to keep going. For Chipo's sake and ours,' she whispered.

Chiedza nodded, but as she continued working, she knew things would never be the same again. Chipo was gone and nothing could bring her back.

After they finished eating their meal, Chiedza and her mother quickly cleaned up the kitchen. Mhondi was already waiting by the door and gestured impatiently for them to hurry.

'Let's go!' he said gruffly. 'We have a lot of work to do in the fields today.'

Chiedza and her mother sighed with exhaustion. They had been up since dawn and the day was already promising to be a long and difficult one, but they knew it was better not to complain. Mhondi was not a man to be trifled with, especially when it came to work. Together, they set off towards the fields.

While they were on their way to the fields, Mhondi lectured them on the importance of hard work and diligence.

'The fields won't tend themselves,' he repeated. 'We must work from dawn till dusk to ensure a good harvest.'

Chiedza and her mother listened in silence, with their eyes fixed on the ground as expected of them to do as women. They knew the routine very well.

After a while, they arrived at the fields where the maize crops stretched out before them. Mhondi handed out the tools and they began to work. Chiedza felt numb as they worked, but as the morning wore on, the physical labour began to take its toll. Her back ached, her hands were raw and her throat was parched. She glanced over at her mother who was working tirelessly beside her.

When the sun reached its peak, Chiedza's father called out for a break. They all collapsed under the shade of a nearby tree exhausted. Her mother pulled out a gourd of water and handed it to Chiedza who drank greedily. Her mother then took a turn drinking from the gourd before handing it back to Chiedza.

While they rested, Chiedza's thoughts turned back to her sister again. The pain of her loss still felt like a fresh wound.

Noticing her distraction, Mhondi frowned. 'Chiedza, you need to focus,' he said sternly. 'We have a lot of work to do.'

Chiedza nodded and they all went back to the field. The day wore on and the sun beat down relentlessly sucking the moisture from the earth. Chiedza's throat was parched, her muscles ached and her skin burned. She felt like she was being consumed by the merciless sun – her strength ebbing away with each passing moment.

Just when she thought she couldn't take it anymore, her father called out for the day to end. They all stumbled back to their homestead exhausted.

They saw a figure waiting by the kitchen's door long before they reached their homestead. His presence was as unwelcome as a viper in the grass. It was Old Nhamo, the old man who had brought the news of Chipo's death. Chiedza's heart skipped a beat as Old Nhamo approached them. *What did he want now?*

Old Nhamo cleared his throat and said, 'The chief has sent a message regarding Chiedza's marriage to his son.'

Mhondi nodded with an expressionless face. 'We are aware of the arrangement.'

Old Nhamo continued, 'The chief has decreed that the marriage will take place in two months from now out of respect for your family's mourning period as per our traditions.'

Chiedza felt a shiver run down her spine as she processed the news. *Two months?* That's all she had left before her life would change forever.

Her mother nodded with her eyes cast downwards. 'We will prepare her for marriage,' she said.

Chiedza felt a feeling of resentment. *Prepare her?* She was already being treated like a commodity – a prize to be presented to the chief's son.

Chiedza's father turned to Old Nhamo. 'Thank you, Old Nhamo. Allow me to walk with you back to the chief's homestead,' he said. 'I've a matter of importance to discuss with him.'

He handed the hoe he had been holding to his wife. He walked alongside Old Nhamo, continuing their conversation as they walked away. Chiedza and her mother watched the two men walk away until they were out of sight. With the day's toil in the fields finally at an end, they carefully returned the worn hoes to their designated resting place, a sturdy wooden rack nestled in the shade of the hut. The tools, their weathered handles worn smooth by generations of use, settled into their accustomed slots with a soft clatter, their iron blades glinting dully in the fading light.

With the hoes safely stowed, they set off towards the river. They worked together filling the clay pots to the brim and walked back home. They both slipped into the warm golden light of their hut when the sun had dipped over the horizon. The scent of wood smoke and simmering stew enveloped them like a gentle hug. With practiced ease, they began to prepare supper. Chiedza helped chop the vegetables and gave them to her mother as she watched her cook. Her mother slid a heavy clay pot onto the cooking fire, its contents a rich flavourful stew made with tender chunks of meat and the fresh vegetables Chiedza had chopped.

Just as they were finishing cooking the evening meal, the sound of footsteps echoed outside growing louder with each passing moment. The hut's entrance was filled with a warm golden light as Chiedza's father stepped across the threshold and sat on his stool. The aroma of simmering stew and freshly cooked pap wafted up mingling with the scent of wood smoke.

With the meal finally ready, Tamburai started dishing for her husband while Chiedza knelt before Mhondi as he washed his hands from the water basin she was holding. Chiedza's mother knelt beside Chiedza and handed her husband the wooden bowls ladled with a decidedly more substantial serving of generous portions of the steaming stew and pap. As the man of the homestead, it was expected that he would receive the largest and most generous portion as a symbol of his status and authority.

Chiedza and her mother received smaller portions. Their bowls were filled with only a small portion of pap and a sparse serving of stew. This was not a matter of preference, but rather a deep ingrained societal expectation – one that Chiedza's mother had grown accustomed to over the years.

They ate in silence, with their eyes cast down at their food as Chiedza's father enjoyed his larger serving. After finishing their meal, Chiedza's father pushed his bowl away with a look of satisfaction on his face. He stood up, retreated to where he slept in the other hut, and lay down on his favourite spot on the reed mat, his eyes closing in contentment.

Chiedza and her mother worked in silence after eating. They gathered the empty bowls and utensils to wash them. They washed the dishes and rinsed them before setting them to dry. Once the cleaning was done, they sat down watching the dying embers on the cooking fire. After a while, they both decided it was time to sleep.

Chiedza walked to her hut. She entered her hut, closing the door behind her. The interior was simple with a reed mat spread out on the floor. She lay down on the mat, wrapping herself in her covering to ward off the chill of the night. She closed her eyes, listening to the crickets and the distant howling of hyenas. As she drifted off to sleep, she thought of her sister, her mother's instructions and her father's stern expression as well as his expectations of her. Her eyelids grew heavy and heavier, making her thoughts grow jumbled and unclear. With that, she fell asleep. The sounds of the night faded into the distance.

Girlz Have Voices Books

- The Angry Girlchild
- Paida
- Women Exceed Poetry Anthology Series
- Paida & Patie, Inspirational Book Series
- Genetic Twists
- Simphlets, Motivational Book Series
- Inspired, Inspirational Book Series
- Mind Over Matter, An Anthology of Poems

facebook.com/girlzhavevoices
INSTAGRAM: @girlzhavevoices
X: @girlzhavevoices
***YouTube*:** Girlz Have Voices

From Darling Kind Publishing

By Tatenda Charles Munyuki
- LOTANDO UREY: The Torture Chamber
- LOTANDO UREY: Servitude Defined
- The Naked Teenager
- GREEN ROSES: Petals and Thorns
- Paida
- The Angry Girlchild
- NACH (Children's Book Series)
- THE MONTE CHICKS (Teenage Book Series)
- BATTLE OF SEXES (Women's Book Series)
- PUSHERZ (Mature Book Series)
- AGENTS (Intelligence Book Series)
- AUSTRALIAN iDOLL Book Series
- OXFORD OXTAILS Book Series
- THE SCOTTISH LASSIES Book Series
- BELFASTING Book Series
- THE CHINESE LETTER Book Series
- MELODIES OF TORONTO Book Series

By Paidamoyo Norman, Patience Mbiriri
- PAIDA & PATIE (Girls and Women's Inspirational Series)

By Simphiwe Ndabazokufa
- SIMHPLETS (Motivational Book Series)

By Christine T Nhamo
- INSPIRED (Inspirational Book Series)

By Anesu Mukombiwa
- Genetic Twists

By Reynold Sibanda
- IDENTITY QUEST: The Dark Path

By Prosper Wilton Makara
- Perfect Imperfections
- The Hashtag Revolution

By Victoria Mundopa
- When You Are Gone

FOR MORE INFORMATION
WhatsApp number: +263737283187
email: tcmpublishing@gmail.com, darlingkindp@live.com
facebook.com/tcmpublishingzim

www.ingramcontent.com/pod-product-compliance
Lightning Source LLC
Chambersburg PA
CBHW061317040426
42444CB00010B/2683